M000207507

This Edge of Rain

This Edge of Rain

Poems by

Jane Ebihara

Jane Ebihara

Donna,
So happy today
to see you
Jane

© 2021 Jane Ebihara. All rights reserved.
This material may not be reproduced in any form, published, re-
printed, recorded, performed, broadcast,
rewritten or redistributed without
the explicit permission of Jane Ebihara.
All such actions are strictly prohibited by law.

Cover design by Shay Culligan
Author photograph by Julie Maloney
Thanks to Dave Hoefler @davehoefler
for making this photo available freely on Unsplash

ISBN: 978-1-63980-049-0

Kelsay Books
502 South 1040 East, A-119
American Fork, Utah 84003
Kelsaybooks.com

for my sons

Acknowledgments

Grateful acknowledgment is made to the following publications in which some of the poems in this collection first appeared:

Edison Literary Review: "If Someday"
Exit 13 Magazine: "Abundance"
Frost Meadow Review: "Pandemic, April 2020"
Offline (South Mountain Poets): "Two Moments"
Paterson Literary Review: "Driving Home in the Rain"
Red River Book of Haibun: "Living Alone," "Tai Chi for Seniors"
Schuylkill Valley Journal: "Widow"
Sonic Boom: "Night Travel"
The Stillwater Review: "To the Doe Nursing Her Fawn in the
    Middle of the Road," "Who Am I to Change the World?"
Tiferet: "A New Season," "Waiting for a Poem"
U.S.1 Worksheets: "At the Corner"

"Advice from the Wildflower," and "Saving the Magnolia" were published in *On The Verge:Poets of the Palisades, III (* The Poet's Press, 2020).

"Last Kiss" was published in *A Constellation of Kisses (Terrapin Press, 2019),* featured on *The Slowdown,* podcast of former U.S. Poet Laureate, Tracy K. Smith.

"If Someday," "Perspective," and "Two Moments" were published in *A Little Piece of Mourning* (Finishing Line Press, 2014).

"A New Season," "To the Doe Nursing Her Fawn in the Middle of the Road," and "Waking Widowed" were published in *A Reminder of Hunger and Wings* (Finishing Line Press, 2019).

Contents

"Would that life were like the shadow cast by a wall or a tree, but it is like the shadow of a bird in flight."

—Talmud

I

Driving Home in the Rain

It was reasonable at first. Tapped the windshield, obscured the gray evening. At Gratitude Farm on 94 the sign is still visible though pond and field have already coupled. Farther down—Yellow Frame Presbyterian and Wilber's Country Store preface the deluge. Turning onto 519 only the taillights of the pick-up in front of me hold me to my proper lane. Still, what beauty blurs beyond. You would have loved this countryside, this place where I now live. I am the daughter you'd remember as the cautious one, but look how I move with confidence though the double yellow line is lost in the storm. I'm still not the country girl you wanted me to be, but I want you to know how I share your love of the land—want to wrap myself in these fields, bathe in loam and the fruit of the plough. I regret you didn't live long enough to know me now. I'm sorry too I didn't stop back there on Long Bridge Road where a little miracle occurred—if I had gotten out of the car I could have straddled that yellow line and with arms outstretched stood halfway in rain and half in dry night air. From that edge of rain, I could have seen the hills lift above the sodden field.

My Mother Never Climbed a Tree

My mother never climbed a tree
or pressed a flower in a book

Never swam naked in the lake
or beat a drum

My mother never sang in the shower
or touched tongues with a lover

Never spared a spider
or sipped a beer

She never wrote a love letter
or watched an eclipse

My mother never drove too fast
or laughed too loud or ate too much

Never climbed a mountain
or rode a bike

My mother never slept with a cat
or flew a kite

She didn't paddle a canoe
build a snowman or ride in a parade

My mother never bared her breasts to the sun

Some of this is true
The rest is also true

Mr. Weir's Market

We are our memories, we are that surreal museum of
inconsistent forms, that pile of broken mirrors.
                              —Jorge Luis Borges

Why this?

A day, mid-recipe,
when my mother fills my pocket
with coins and sends me on my bike
to Mr. Weir's Market.

A day I pedal up the alley between
Calhoun and Clay to the little shelter
behind his house—

a quiet knock to unlock the store.

The day he shuffles to the shelf, lifts down
the tin of baking powder or was it cinnamon,
dusts it off a bit and takes the coins from
my opened palm.

The day penny change buys a pink
Bazooka for the ride home—
a tiny cartoon tucked inside.

Why this as memory and not
the senior prom or the color of
my first love's eyes?

Instead, this relic:
a child, a blue three-speed,
an old man, silent and stooped,
an alley, a knock, a dusty tin.
And what of this late Winter day
that seems now to remember Spring?

Two Moments

in the ladies' room

      she lifts her shirt

caresses her belly

      swollen   tight   round

he kicks   rolls   presses

      against the wall of her abdomen

pulses toward her fingers

      splayed wide in warm embrace

soon he will know *blue*

      the touch of fingertips to lips

she will teach him

      soft   *sky*   *mother*   *universe*   *goodbye*

and he will leave his stories pressed

      into the palm of her outstretched hand

To the Doe Nursing Her Fawn
in the Middle of the Road

love is no sister to common sense
hunger not even a distant cousin
we mean to be careful mothers
yet have all thrown caution aside
in the name of desire

I have made my own foolish choices
fueled by what wells
swollen and throbbing inside
that which I offered up as devotion
often too in unlikely places

Waiting for a Poem

stare at the empty page

watch the young buck
the soft fur of his antlers
lift and lower in the daisies
        give him wings

listen to the dove whistle *danger*
and to the jay's alarm

imagine your father beside you
hearing all the words you never spoke

press your face to the lilacs that once
lined your grandmother's lane
        bring some home

watch the turkey poults with their mother—
sentry on the daily visit—
        tell her you understand

recall a lover's head on your chest
his hand tracing the curve of your hip

let the morning sun rest on your shoulder
and the clouded sky swaddle

touch the damp earth
        who weeps

for the rising seas
for the children
the fallen
the burning
the mute

pick up your pen

A Man with Earth for Blood
Morning for Muscle

for my father

be still he said
be still and if you listen
you will hear
a wing beat   an insect feed
an earthworm root in the soil

be still he said
be still and watch

and you will see a sponge of morel beside the elm
that marbled fish at water's edge
wings caught in a silken web

he believed in God and heaven too he said
just in case

what was there to do
on the day of his last breath when
strangers carried the body away

but go to his garden
touch the earth
taste the tomato straight from the vine
listen for a quiet song

Brother

this is a poem about a silence

not sleeping-child silence
not blaze-of-sunrise silence
not burst-of-milkweed or
moth wing silence

this poem is about absence
         the empty room after
         the door is closed

this is a poem about the buried
the unspoken

about a child who once was
then never was

it's what everyone did back then they tell me—
you just picked yourself up and went on

packed away memories
even his name

it's the way it was done

we had the same parents
he and I
         except we did not

mine had only daughters
and a secreted sorrow
his had new love
and their firstborn son

this is a poem about the silence
of two syllables withheld
like a breath

If Someday

I am dying
>do not lay your head upon my chest to listen
>do not ask me questions I can no longer answer
>do not allow those who never knew me to speak for me

instead
>resuscitate only memory
>>take me to the window
>>>show me the sunset
>>>even if I no longer know what beauty is

>>whisper in my ear
>>>the names of children
>>>even if I no longer know how to love

>>touch me
>>>with those hands like small birds
>>>even if I can no longer feel the dance

>>play *My Romance*
>>>and remember ours
>>>>before we say goodbye

The Belly of the Goose

I walk under a
cool October sky   recall
those other autumn days when

little boys then
you pedaled home from play

I can hear the rustle of nylon wind-breakers
the squeak of sneakers
smell the sweat of tousled hair

time I think
time I say to the closing day

overhead
a flock of geese   low
in fading copper light
tear me from my reverie

I reach up
want to touch those
warm beating breasts

but they fly too high
out of reach
disappear

Saving the Magnolia

fish knife in hand
my neighbor Blanca
is up in the tree again

an insect has found weakness
in her magnolia whose
strong fleshy petals unfold in spring
like a woman turned inside-out

headscarf tied around gray hair
Blanca balances
ready for battle   she scrapes
scrapes and vows to stop the intruder

the parasitic scale sucks sap—
hatches its young beneath
a homely waxen blanket

                                    nearby
a house wren gathers fern and twigs
feathers a swallow's nest claimed
as her own

a gravid cowbird waits

A Sorry State

I have spent my whole life saying *sorry*
someone drives a grocery cart into my backside
sorry
the bill is four-thirty-six
sorry I only have a twenty

my apolojectis needs to be removed

bequeathed by my mother this organ
leaves me feeling responsible
for anything that goes wrong in the universe

I've apologized to doors I've walked into
      to listeners when the word I need is lost
      to people I've never met for not knowing their names
      to my dog for getting in his way and
      to Alexa for asking her to repeat the time

I need it to rain on a picnic without feeling I chose the wrong day
I want no-fault sneezes and hiccups

post apolojectomy I'll finally be free
to remain silent when something goes wrong

unless of course it's my fault
      sorry I didn't mention that

A Visitor

I didn't visit often
she a thousand miles away
so when I arrived I announced myself
no quiz imposed since I'd been warned
Mother, it's your daughter, Jane

she was delighted   all smiles
decked out in the red felt hat
I had sent for birthday ninety-seven
we talked   laughed   reminisced
       Daddy hunting morels
       Uncle Willie's ragout
       my grandson's blue blue eyes

I pushed her chair around the grounds
almost to the cornfield nearby
'til the distance worried her some

and when it was time to go
she took my hand   my mother
sought my gaze with watered eyes
and said
       if *I ever have children*
       I'll name a daughter Lily
       after you

Summer Days

scorch of hot tar on bare feet
shock of sprinkler spray
flickering firefly nights
bottle caps gathered from gutters
tire swing under the walnut tree
lemonade for a nickel

~

sparkle of lake water
hot earth in the hand
turtle crossing the road
an indigo bird with wings aflame
singe of sunset
leaves of a burning bush

II

Poets All

...what would be wrong with a world in which everybody were writing poems?

—Ted Kooser

Imagine everyone a poet.

All the cars on the off ramp driven by poets, poets palming plums in the market, the plumber under your sink—poet. The doctor with stethoscope to your chest, the politician, the policeman on the corner, the child in the sprinkler, the one picking dandelions in the field. The homeless man asleep on the sidewalk, the farmer on the plow, the post-man, the priest.

Poets all.

What if everyone were paying attention—
        pausing for cricket song, starlight,
        sorrow, storm, the wail
        of sax in a subway tunnel?

What if everyone weeded words
        until only the perfect remained?

Would the globe be warmed with words,
        littered with song?

Would time be lavished watching
        a man tie his father's shoe,
                a vulture soar through growing light,
                a meteor fall,
                        a willow sway?

Would everyone listen—
      hear the cries of the broken,
                    the forgotten,
                            the lost?

Perfect Pitch

*Most blind people move within the confines of the blind
world, and never leave that comfort zone, but I was never that way.*
—Juan Pablo Culasso
Newark, NJ Star Ledger, June 12, 2016

he *sees*
birds through song   knows
three thousand strong

hears beauty
in the music of the Antarctic—
     seals and sea lion
     the melody of melting ice

his sightless world
symphony

he records
     the hush of sunset
     hymns from the throats of thrush

names each note made
when a tossed stone
hits the river

At the Corner

He approached me at the corner of West 79th and Amsterdam—not palm up, but with a simple request: would I buy him some vegetables. Could have been a sudden unexpected storm, a bus jumping the curb, a spaceship landing for the speechless response his plea evoked. He gave me his eyes. I gave him my stunned silence. And in those seconds he was gone. Faded into the face of the city. There are thousands of names for regret, I answer to them all.

Widow

for Sue

it wasn't supposed to end like this
he is supposed to be at the kitchen door
dripping with garden gifts
Sweetness, where'd you put the hummer food?

he gardens still
down at the Prairie City cemetery
where bagpipe strains of *Amazing Grace*
hang heavy in the country air

gardens now like that giant
composter he loved
that sits under the pine tree doing its quiet work

his ragged fishing cap hangs
on the hall tree hook
and the tracks of his garden boots paint
the floor in front of his favorite chair
the one in which the cat now curls alone
selfish with sorrow

no use shaking a fist at God
she curses him instead
head bowed in the rose garden
the sweet pea patch   the calla lilies—
the white ones he took with him to the grave

curses him with fists of weeds
damn you it wasn't supposed to end like this
tears are not enough to do this work

37

March 2003
Still Counting

every day
an old man snails his way past my kitchen window
his face lost in the hood of his bulky jacket
his cane taps out each step—recalls
the cadence of combat
one   two   one   two

I watch
wash remnants
of chicken soup from our bowls
allow my hands a warm bath in soapy water
the radio reports the latest count
twenty-six Americans dead
   twenty-two British dead
      seven missing

somewhere a wife   a husband
    a father   a mother   a child
counts
one   one   one

Unforeseen

the man I married first—
        father to my sons
didn't wake this morning
died
the way we all say we want to—
peacefully in sleep

our grandson runs his five-year-old forefinger
over the rimples of my neck
says, *Nana, I'm tracing this map*

I know those roads
those intersections   turns   dead-ends
drawn now on this neck

of a once-young woman
who loved and left
forty-three years ago

I'm tracing this map

what resurrection
this death evokes

what startling sorrow

Looking for a Poem
Somewhere Near Pittsburgh

I sat on a balcony
overlooking a Days Inn pool
and made a list titled

NOTES FROM A BALCONY

a fleshy woman smooths lotion on an ample thigh
a tissue-pale lifeguard perches over an empty pool
an old man thaws chicken legs on a portable grill

I watched from above like some hungry goddess
unseen in the unquiet
the carnival of characters my feast

a tattooed woman with a frizzy red bob
a bearded young man splayed on a plastic chaise
a couple arguing two chairs apart

it's been years since I watched them
as they played at something close to pleasure
where

rubber sandals slapped the gray cement
a jet passed overhead
a ragged American flag decayed in the sun

Unremarkable

This is not the morning
yolks break in the pan

and clouds hang low over
distant hills.

This is not the morning
dogwood blossoms fall,

the car runs out of gas,
or the clay cup in my hand

takes me away to
a day when devotion was
a gift I thought would
never break.

This is not the morning
the ambulance comes,
the doctor calls,
the letter arrives.

This is a morning
when nothing breaks,

nothing dies.

Memories lie quiet in their shells,
deer gather on the lawn,

the cup in my hand
simply a cup.

Perspective

while we sleep
bellies full
on our soft clean sheets

the night fills
with hunger   with want

last night
deer ate the roses
the newly born asters   the sunflowers
and that blood-red mystery bud

ours are not the dreams of the starving
the nightmares of the thirsty who
stagger worlds away toward
another morning

we who have never known such want
wake   curse what creeps in the dark
touches soft lips to thorns
and devours the very things
we meant to love

Confession 2015

the woman checking out next to me
at Discount Drugs juggles fourteen bottles
of anti-bacterial hand soap

I know this is crazy
but my son uses an entire one of these every day
I think he's a little OCD
but I gave it to him—always telling him
      it's flu season
            don't touch anything
               wash your hands
you never know what you might get from someone

I have to pay for these with cash for a crazy reason
she tells both the clerk and me
her secrets running away from home now

it's clear
she cannot let her husband know
just how infectious
a mother's love can be

Spaces

bottom of the top hat
where the rabbit hides

empty place you can't
stop your tongue from probing

gap where your finger slips and curls
to guide the tea cup to your lips

break between moving branches
where blue sky quiets

abyss where we toss
the penny and the wish

endless void between us
thick with thoughts
unspoken

Late Autumn

Just yesterday the tree against the window
blazed in dusky light.
Autumn-rusted leaves graced the view.

Today the tree's stripped limbs arch
over a swell of faded pageantry—
burnt copper   tangerine   russet   bronze.

Summoning the alphabet I struggle
to recall the tree's name—reach
the D's and the tree is a dogwood again.

I've been losing words. Not just names of
trees or people I once knew, but names
 of things—
            kitchen tongs   nuthatch
            wheelbarrow   artichoke—

words I could do without, no doubt,
but winter nears—exposes
a horizon summer conceals.

Spring will return to soften the landscape, still
there is no word to stop the leaving.

This is what the seasons give,
lessons in the language of loss.

Aubade

the old woman in my mirror craves
little more now
than kinship with the living

she claims sisterhood with every fleeting thing
     slug and sparrow
     mite and minx
     seed and spore
     beetle and bear
         the mighty and minuscule

the woman in the mirror savors
fire   laughter   the longed-for song
and language not her own

she leaves her meal
on the table
growing cold

hungers only
for morning
     then morning again

III

The Earth Tilts

and autumn
unfolds the last bounty
gilds all in yellow light
      haystack
      fallen leaf
      fallow field
dry reminders of
      what was

autumn
governed by light
charms like a feckless lover
bearing gifts
makes no promise of
      what will be

Waking Widowed

four seasons now
still that slap of reality
with each dawn
it is so   it is really so
even my bed is a startling
          unfamiliar field

nightmares fade in the day's light
truth does not
widow   I am a widow
the word itself sounds broken

widow the word a printer says
doesn't fit on a page
rests alone on the next
leftover

the widow
something   not someone

in forty years
not once did I wake to the thought
I am married
how many seasons
before I wake without the wound

widows no longer wear black
we wear a different costume
one that feels stolen
from another woman's closet

a gown that falls
heavily on the body
like an unanswered question
which one of us is gone

Sorting

housebound for the fourth Nor'easter of the month
I decide it's time to cull my spices

it's spring   still
frigid winds empty snowy boughs
onto the already burdened yard

inside I empty shelves of gummy tins
and bottles—some of which I'm sure came
with me from marriage one—over forty years ago

I shake garlic powder   cloves   parsley
and onion flakes into the trash—
tribute to innocence and culinary ignorance
to a time of tuna casseroles
torn from the pages of Women's Day
Hamburger Helper and boxed mac'n cheese—
what I called cooking then

nothing lasts
the snow piles

I add remnants of marriage two
Hungarian paprika   garam masala   five spice bouquet
to the growing mound

all relationships end
in divorce   death   desertion

roasted sesame seeds   dill weed
peppercorns   marjoram   sage
something called "Joe's Stuff"   unopened
at what point in my life was that a good idea

winds whip the snow to drifts

empty containers rinsed and ready to recycle
line up across the counter
flavors faded by time

it will be fresh herbs now and spices
purchased with purpose
carefully seasoned meals
for one

A New Season

this is not a poem about autumn

though you might guess so if you
saw me writing here
      in quiet woods
      while a soft breeze loosens
            another sycamore leaf

      where squirrels skitter and skeetch
            over mounds of fallen pine needles
            follow a fading memory

this is not a poem about death

      though soon these woods
      will announce the strange
      loveliness of leaving
      with a riot of red and gold

you left me in autumn
you have never left me
both will always be so

this is not a poem about you

I've spread those poems across
the endless nights   now
I'm weary of ruin
alone

I am alone
that may always be so

this is not a poem about me

the lake is alive now
sun and wind play on the surface

I am alive
watch a new season arrive

sometimes
this is how
a love poem
ends

Caress

an old woman in
summer gown

listens to the rain
tap tap on
          leaf and limb
          stone and lawn

and is drawn
to the open door

steps into the night
bare arms outstretched

gives herself to the
soft touch offered only

by this summer rain

Night Travel

I am in a helicopter piloted either by my first husband (the one I divorced) or the second (the one who died.) Neither of them can fly. It's unclear which one is behind the controls at any given time. One nearly slams us into a mountain and the other insists without words that to fly through subway tunnels and under bridges is safer than the sky. Metal blades rattle and scrape on the tunnel walls. Slice away at the bridge above. My writing folder tips,

and loose pages flutter
away through walls
that are no longer there.

Pandemic
April 2020

eliminate all non-essential travel
stay six feet away from others wear
a mask in public stay home stay
home the virus doesn't move we do
stay home wash your hands stay
home wash your hands don't touch
your face stay home

from home—
our sanctuaries and cells—
we long for the ordinary
    a haircut. a gathering the
gym a carwash a night out
    an embrace

I stand at the window looking out
                        looking out

in April wind
a long abandoned nest
no bigger than a teacup
clings to the dogwood

a male cardinal at the feeder lifts
seeds to the beak of his mate
three turkey vultures swoop low
cast shadows on the lawn

Advice from the Wildflower

push

through the darkness
until it breaks around you

open

yourself to the sun

become

the light you seek

do this

no matter where you fall
no matter who gardens there

Another Today

for the fourth time since your last breath
the calendar has turned to May

the dogwood outside the kitchen window blooms
the neighbors' cherry too   those neighbors
you never trusted   never knew

not much has changed
everything has changed

I've grown accustomed to your absence
my life all mine   our life all mine

had the driveway resurfaced   the deck re-stained
got a new desk chair   a potted plant
learned to use all your remotes   well most

you know how they say *life goes on*
it does

sometimes when the house is dark and still
I play the piano in the loft
imagine you below
listening

sometimes
I ask you questions I know the answers to

I am no longer your wife
I am the woman I might have been
if I'd never been your wife

                    no
that's not true

I am the woman who was your wife
the one who begins again each day

the wind blows now

dogwood and cherry blossoms
drift like snow

if you were here
I'd call you to the window

Abundance

he wanted to find duck eggs
       not under the duck
       but close
he wanted to wander country roads
see a faded sign tacked to a fence post
a battered cooler roadside

he wanted to inquire at local haunts
test his theory that when asked where
one could buy duck eggs everyone would respond
I've seen a sign—just don't know where—

and he'd turn and smile
see I told you in his eyes then

return to the road—always the one less traveled—
charmed by the response
encouraged by the possibility

there's a sign out there somewhere

he wanted duck eggs
so we roamed

past bare fields scattered with hay bales
       geometry of spring
past the grazing horses goats cows and sheep
past the forgotten cottage with its own story to tell
past the cemetery of toppled stones washed by time

and we found them

safe in a farmer's milk house
presented to us like miracles of light
a heft in the palm

and later
cracked in a skillet hot
and seductive as rising suns

Living Alone

It's good I have extra rooms in my house for it is filling up with words. No one to call to the window for the splash of goldfinch at the feeder, the doe in the garden. *Yellow, still, quiet, delight* fall in fractured syntax—pile in the corner. Laments and unasked questions stashed in bags line the hallway walls. Stuffed kitchen cabinets spew complete sentences onto the counter tops. Nouns, verbs, adjectives, invectives, useless articles fall behind cushions and topple from shelves that can no longer bear the weight.

One day my children will discover this mess—call in an expert in such matters who will survey the premises and ask in gentle tones if I really need the box of synonyms for regret. She'll say *you can keep the ones you must, but you can always get new ones.* They'll strip everything down to the essentials.

> when the last woman steps
> into the quiet wood
> what language will fall
> in her wake

Who Am I to Change the World

all is broken
and it's been raining for days

        oil spills
        crowded slums
        an ocean of plastic

my husband is dead

        ice caps melt
        red tides grow
        war looms

the garden is full of weeds

what can I do

        factory farming
        overfishing
        the children   the children

our ship is sinking
fool at the helm

still
a new season comes
leaves pile   decay
in silence I can hear them letting go

I have a rake

Tai Chi for Seniors

Our instructor teaches us *Repel the Monkey* and *Dragon Serves Tea.* Shows us how this poetry translates into self-defense. *Snake Sticks Out Its Tongue* he says and in flawless motion we lift and reach with aged palms. *Hands Wave Like Clouds* and we respond in unison—seven women who know clouds like these will never save us. Could we summon *Golden Crane Stands on One Leg* if a handbag were snatched on a subway platform? Or *Grasp the Swallow's Tail* in a dark parking lot? Our teacher believes we will. We know it is enough—this learning how to breathe, how to balance, how to fall.

Last Kiss

First, in your seventies and alone, you read that those who
count such things say an average person kisses for a total

of two weeks in a lifetime. And you realize your two weeks
was up some time ago. Suddenly there is kissing everywhere

you look. And you learn that cows kiss and squirrels. Puffins,
snails and meerkats! And you are overcome with sorrow and

an overwhelming desire to kiss—to be kissed. And you learn
that's called basorexia and you have it. You watch the lips

of strangers in the supermarket—wonder if one would want
to kiss you. You know now that a minute of kissing burns

twenty-six calories and that a man lives up to five years
longer if he kisses his lover before he goes to work. You want

to tell someone that. And what's worse, unlike the first kiss,
the last slipped by unnoticed. It might have been

a spring day when daffodils answered the sun's invitation or
an autumn day when everything else was burning. Or simply

a day you took out the garbage, did a load of wash. Then, someone
comes and takes your hand and you remember words

to a song you thought you'd never hear again and you remember
all those sunsets you forgot to watch and the smell of woods in rain.

And you remember the river, the river—how it presses
its mouth again and again to the swollen sea

About the Author

Born and raised in Illinois, Jane Ebihara has lived in New Jersey since 1977. After receiving a B.S. Ed from Western Illinois University and a M.S. Ed from Rutgers University, she taught middle school literature in Roxbury Township, NJ, for twenty-six years. As a result of a workshop for teachers offered by the Geraldine Dodge Foundation, Jane was awarded a fellowship to attend The Fine Arts Workshop in Provincetown, MA, and also began a poetry group of fellow teacher/poets which has met monthly for over twenty years.

Jane has been a Pushcart Prize nominee and is the author of two chapbooks, *A Little Piece of Mourning* (Finishing Line Press, 2014) and *A Reminder of Hunger and Wings* (Finishing Line Press, 2019). She has been a volunteer writer for New Jersey NORWESCAP's Senior Life Stories Project and currently serves as an Associate Editor of *The Stillwater Review* and Poetry Contest Editor of *Tiferet*.

She resides in rural Warren County, New Jersey and can be contacted on her web page or by email.

www.janeebihara.com
jeeb@optonline.net